```
J                R593229
629.2               8.30
Bar
Barrett
Motorcycles
```

DATE DUE			
MY 18 '93	DE 7 '94		
SE 3 '93			
SE 22 '93			
DE 27 '93	R 3 '95		
FE 25 '94	AG 30 '95		
MY 20 '94			
JY 20 '94			
AG 24 '94			
SE 14 '94			
SE 21 '94			

PICTURE LIBRARY
Motorcycles

N. S. Barrett

Franklin Watts

London   New York   Sydney   Toronto

© 1984 Franklin Watts Ltd

First published in Great Britain
   1984 by
Franklin Watts Ltd
12a Golden Square
London W1

First published in the USA by
Franklin Watts Inc
387 Park Avenue South
New York
N.Y. 10016

First published in Australia by
Franklin Watts
1 Campbell Street
Artarmon, NSW 2064

U.S. ISBN: 0-531-15142-5 (pbk)
US ISBN: 0-531-03783-5
Library of Congress Catalog Card
Number: 84-50017

Designed by
McNab Design

Photographs by
Don Morley

Illustrated by
Tony Bryan

Technical Consultant
Don Morley

Contents

Introduction	6
The motorcycle	8
Racing bikes	10
Sidecars	13
Off the road	14
Working bikes	17
Speedway	18
Ice racing	21
Dragsters	22
Specials	23
Stunt riding	26
The story of bikes	28
Facts and records	30
Glossary	31
Index	32

Introduction

People use motorcycles to get from place to place. They are cheaper to run than cars. They do not get held up so much in heavy traffic and are easier to park.

Motorcycles are a fast means of transport in busy city centers. They are used by the police and messenger services.

△ People ride motorcycles for transportation and pleasure. Protective helmets must always be worn in case of accidents.

Motorcycles are also used in sport. Riders zoom round racing circuits or over rough country on specially made motorcycles.

△ Motorcycle racing is an exciting sport. Riders race around circuits at high speeds.

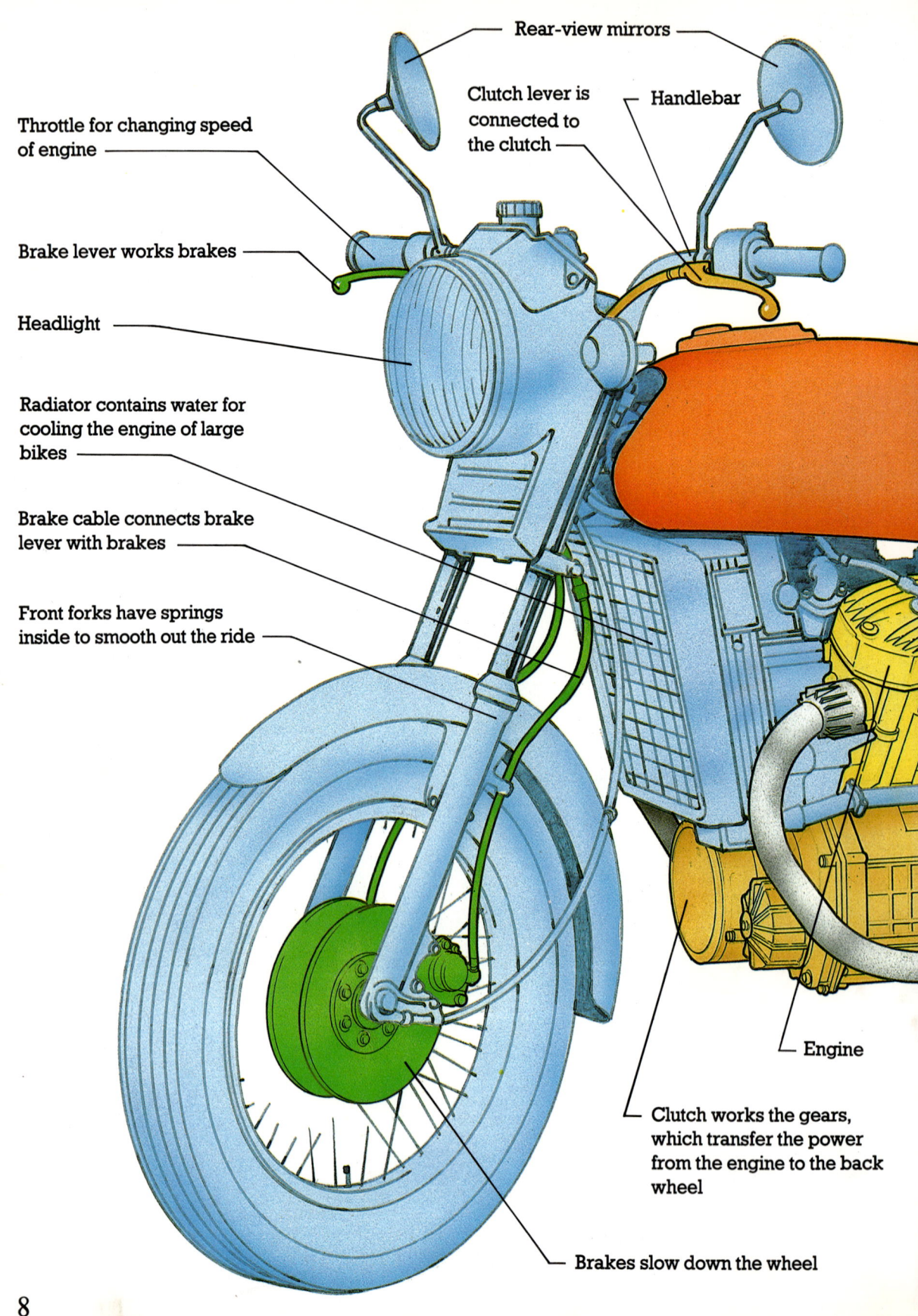

The motorcycle

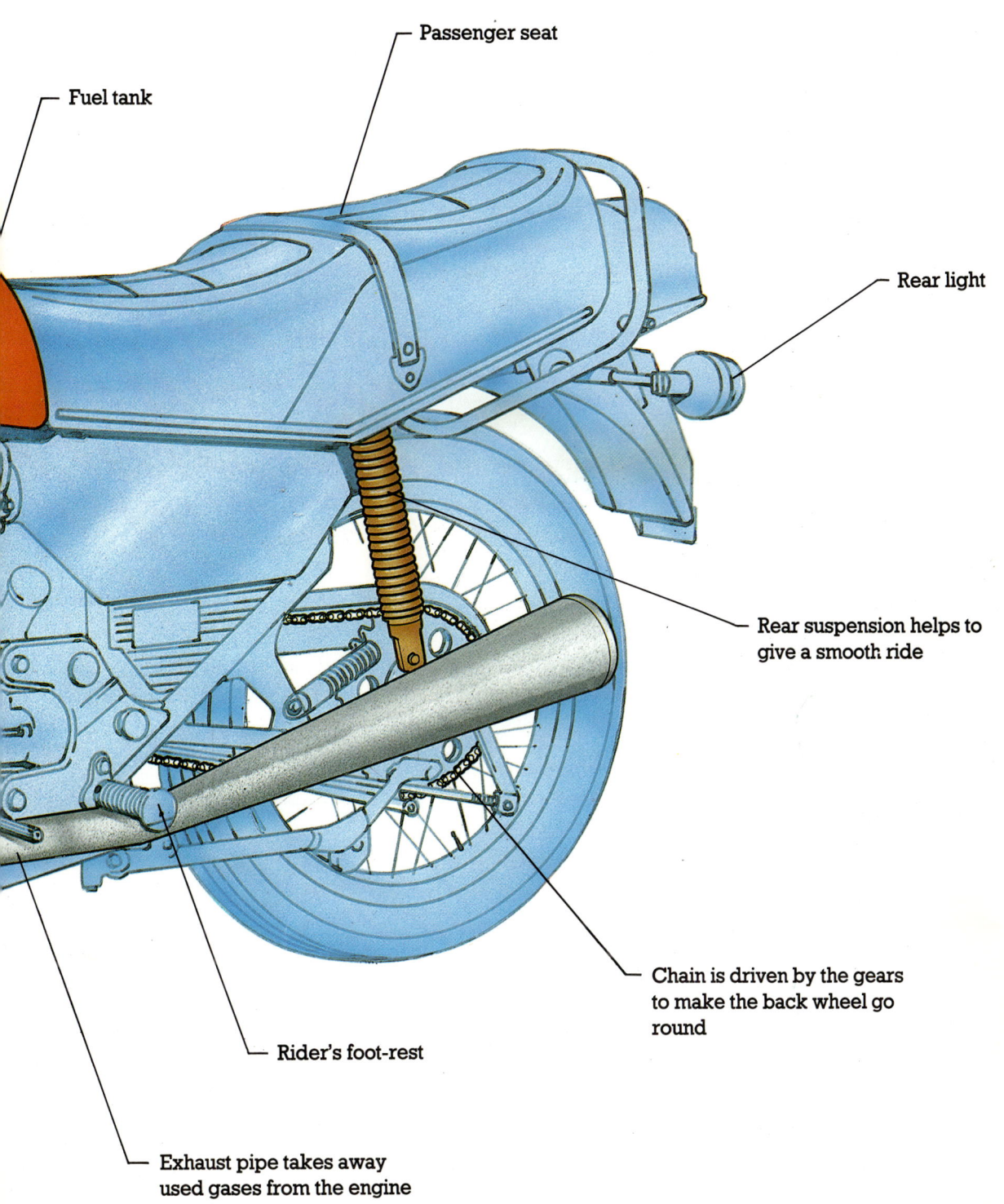

Passenger seat

Fuel tank

Rear light

Rear suspension helps to give a smooth ride

Chain is driven by the gears to make the back wheel go round

Rider's foot-rest

Exhaust pipe takes away used gases from the engine

Racing bikes

Some motorcycles, or "motorbikes," are very fast. Races used to take place on the roads, with ordinary motorbikes. Now most racing is on tracks or special circuits, and the machines are specially built for racing. They can go as fast as 195 mph (315 km/h) on the straight parts of the circuit.

△ Riders prepare for the start of a race. The ones who were fastest in practice line up in the front row of starters.

▷ There are races for different sizes of motorcycles. These are the smallest racing machines, called "80cc." They have small engines and thin wheels.

An important motorcycle race is called a "grand prix." This is French for "big prize." There are several of these exciting races each year in different countries.

The first 10 riders in each race earn points—from 15 for 1st place to 1 for 10th. The rider with the most points in a year is the world champion. Successful riders earn big prizes.

△ Riders wear studded pads on their knees, which often touch the ground when they go around corners. The riders lean inward to keep the bike balanced.

Sidecars

A sidecar is for passengers. It is attached to the side of the motorcycle. A motorcycle and sidecar "combination" has three wheels. It is steadier than the motorcycle by itself.

There are special sidecar events at race events. The racing sidecar combinations are built as one-piece machines.

▽ In sidecar racing the passenger plays an important part. He or she helps to balance the machine. The passenger often has to lean right out, almost touching the ground.

Off the road

Not all motorcycle sport takes place on road circuits. Riders race round special cross-country courses, over rough, muddy ground. This is called "moto-cross," or "scrambling." There are always plenty of steep climbs and sharp turns.

Riders also compete on dirt track ovals called "flat tracks," and in stadium events which have specially built obstacles.

△ Riders set out at the start of a junior moto-cross race. Boys and girls can begin this sport at the age of five.

▷ "Trials riding" is another form of motorcycle sport. Competitors lose points if they put a foot on the ground.

△ In "arena trials," riders are timed over an obstacle course. If they make mistakes, they have a number of seconds added to their time.

◁ Junior moto-cross events are graded by age. Older competitors use larger bikes. The bikes have a knobby tread on the tires for gripping muddy and loose surfaces.

Working bikes

Motorcycles are also used by the police for moving quickly through heavy traffic. They are used by messengers and postal workers. "Topboxes" and boxes at the side called "saddlebags" can be attached for carrying parcels.

△ Doctors often use motorcycles on racing circuits to get to the scene of an accident quickly. In some places, doctors ride motorbikes on their rounds. They are also used to carry urgent supplies of medicine or blood.

Speedway

Speedway is a popular sport in many parts of the world. It began in Australia. Speedway bikes are light and have no gears or brakes.

Four riders race around an oval cinder track. They go around four times—four "laps." The winner earns 3 points, the second 2, and the third 1. Teams compete against each other in speedway matches.

▷ Speedway bikes have no brakes. The riders slide round the bends. This is called "broadsiding."

▽ Getting off to a good start is very important in speedway. As soon as the starting tapes go up, the riders burst out in clouds of smoke and cinders.

△ The cinders fly as the riders fight for the lead on the first bend of a race. They use their left feet on the ground to help balance the bike.

The world's best speedway riders race in Europe. But many world champions have come from the USA, Australia, and New Zealand.

In the USA, dirt tracks are used, and the sport is called "flat-track racing." More than four riders take part. Speedway also takes place on grass and on ice. There is indoor speedway, too, on boards.

Ice racing

△ The start of a race in the World Ice Speedway Championships. Ice racing is popular in Sweden, the USSR and the USA.

◁ Bikes used for ice racing have spikes screwed into the tires. These grip the smooth surface of the track.

Dragsters

Drag races take place over a straight ¼-mile (402 m) track. Riders use special machines called "dragsters." They race in pairs.

A drag race is over in a few seconds. Dragsters often have more than one engine to provide extra power for racing.

△ The start of a drag race. Dragsters have a frame at the back and a wide rear tire to keep them steady.

Specials

Luxury motorcycles such as the American Harley-Davidson can cost more than some cars. They are built for comfort and looks rather than speed. Their owners might fit them with stereo radio or paint them in bright colors. Some people like to rebuild parts of the bike to their own design. This is called "customizing" the bike.

▽ A Harley-Davidson Electra-Glide. This magnificent bike needs a great deal of care to keep it in tip-top condition.

▷ This fantastic vehicle looks like a strange car and trailer. But in fact it is a "customized" motorcycle. Its owner has used a great deal of imagination to build something really special.

Stunt riding

Motorcycle displays are popular before big race events or at special shows. Stunt riders perform daredevil feats, such as taking off to jump over a row of cars. Display teams do tricks on bikes. They might form human pyramids while riding several bikes in a line or crowd as many as possible on to one machine. The record is 22!

△ Eddie Kidd leaps his machine over a line of cars. Stunt riders such as Kidd and Evel Knievel take off from a ramp at high speed.

▷ A display rider jumps his bike off a ramp through a wall of fire. Such stunts are very dangerous. The rider must be highly skilled and wear protective clothing.

The story of bikes

△ A beautifully restored 1903 Anglian motorcycle. The gasoline tank, a separate oil tank and a small engine are fitted to an ordinary bicycle.

The first motorcycles

The first motorcycles were motorized bicycles—that is, ordinary bicycles fitted with a motor. Steam engines were used to begin with. But the first real motorcycle was built by the German inventor Gottlieb Daimler in 1886. He used his new gasoline engine to power it.

The first races

As soon as motorcycles were invented, people began to race on them. The first races took place in Germany and Austria.

For years, racing bikes were ordinary motorcycles. In countries where racing was allowed, it took place on the roads. The most famous events were the Tourist Trophy races. They are still held in the British Isles, and people come from all over the world to watch them.

Building better bikes

Motorcycle designers gradually made improvements, and built faster and better bikes. They made the engine larger and mounted it low and in the center of the bike. They also made the fuel tank bigger, and placed it above the engine. More powerful brakes were used, and suspension and gears were introduced.

Makers of bikes encouraged motorcycle racing. The names of successful makes of bikes became very well known. It was a good test for their machines.

△ A 1927 Norton shows how the motorcycle developed into a more powerful machine.

Motorcycles today

The motorcycles people ride today do not look very different from those of 50 or 60 years ago. But there have been huge improvements in how well they work. Better materials are used, and better fuel and engine design give them much more power. Improved methods of manufacture have made motorcycles more reliable. They are now designed to give the rider and passenger more comfort and safety.

△ A modern road machine, the Honda VF750F. This type of "roadster" is also raced in special events.

Racing motorcycles

Racing motorbikes are built for speed. This is not just for fast speed along a straight track. The motorbikes also have to take the tight twists and turns at fast speeds. The racing bike's shape is "streamlined," by having the body covered with a case called

△ A modern streamlined racing bike, a Suzuki Gamma Racer.

a "fairing." This allows the air to flow past without slowing the bike down.

Choppers

Choppers are bikes with very long front forks and a small front wheel. They are called choppers because they are standard bikes with bits "chopped off" and new bits added. People build choppers because they like their looks and enjoy riding them.

△ A typical "chopper." It is hard to believe that it started off as an ordinary Triumph.

29

Facts and records

△ Don Vesco with his record-breaking two-wheeler *Lightning Bolt*.

World speed record
The world speed record for a two-wheel motorcycle was set by an American, Don Vesco, in 1978. He was fully enclosed in his specially built "streamliner" called *Lightning Bolt*. It looked more like a torpedo than a motorbike. His record speed, set on Bonneville Salt Flats, Utah, was 318.6 mph (512.7 km/h). This was the average of two runs in opposite directions, made at full speed.

Drag record
The speed record for dragsters, made from a standing start, was set by another American, Bo O'Brochta. He covered the ¼-mile (402 m) in 7.08 seconds in 1980.

World Champions
Giacomo Agostini of Italy has won the most World Motorcycle Championships. He was World Motorcycle Champion 15 times. He won 8 Championships in the 500cc class and 7 in the 350cc class.

Ivan Mauger of New Zealand has won the most World Speedway Championships. He was World Champion 6 times.

Glossary

cc
The letters cc stand for "cubic centimeters." This tells you the size of a motorcycle engine. Most small bikes have 50cc engines. Really big bikes have engines of 1000cc or more.

Circuit
A circuit is a race track. Grand Prix motorcycle racing takes place on specially built circuits. All circuits are different. But each circuit has a number of bends and straight sections. A race consists of many "laps" around the circuit.

Fairing
The fairing is the smooth casing that is used to cover the body of a motorbike or a part of it. It gives the bike a smart look and is shaped to help it move faster.

Lap
A lap is once around a circuit.

Saddlebags
The containers attached to the sides of the bike at the back are called saddlebags.

Pillion
The passenger seat on a motorbike is called a pillion.

Road racing
At one time, most racing took place on roads closed to traffic. Now, most road race meetings are held on special circuits.

Slicks
Smooth tires are called "slicks." They are used for road racing in dry weather and for drag racing.

Streamlining
The outside casing (the fairing) and the windshield of a bike are smooth and shaped in a special way. This is called streamlining. It helps to prevent the force of the air from slowing the bike down.

Topbox
A container attached to the top of the bike behind the saddle. It is used for carrying goods.

Tread
The tread is the raised part of the tire that touches the ground. The deeper the tread, the more grip the tire has on wet or muddy surfaces.

Wheelie
When the front wheel of a bike lifts in the air, it is called a "wheelie." It may happen when a rider starts off too fast.

Index

Agostini, Giacomo 30
Anglian 28
arena trials 16

brakes 8
broadsiding 18, 19

cc 31
chain 9
chopper 29
circuit 10, 31
clutch 8
crash helmet 6
customizing 23, 24, 25

Daimler, Gottlieb 28
dragsters 22, 30

engine 8
exhaust pipe 9

fairing 29, 31
flat-track racing 20
forks 8
fuel tank 9

grand prix 12

Harley-Davidson 23
Honda 29

ice racing 21

Kidd, Eddie 26
knee pads 12
Knievel, Evel 26

lap 18, 31

Mauger, Ivan 30
moto-cross 14, 16

Norton 28

O'Brochta, Bo 30

pillion 31

racing bikes 7, 10, 11, 12, 13, 29
radiator 8

saddlebags 17, 31
scrambling 14
sidecars 13
slicks 31
speedway 18, 19, 20, 30
streamlining 29, 31
stunt riding 26, 27
suspension 9
Suzuki 29

throttle 8
topbox 17, 31
Tourist Trophy 28
tread 31
trials riding 15, 16
Triumph 29

Vesco, Don 30

wheelie 31
world champion 12, 30
world speed record 30